# Instant Nginx Starter

Implement the nifty features of nginx
with this focused guide

**Martin Fjordvald**

PUBLISHING

BIRMINGHAM - MUMBAI

# Instant Nginx Starter

First published: April 2013

Production Reference: 1170413

Published by Packt Publishing Ltd.
Livery Place
35 Livery Street
Birmingham B3 2PB, UK.

ISBN 978-1-78216-512-5

www.packtpub.com

# Credits

**Author**

Martin Fjordvald

**Reviewers**

José Miguel Parrella

Michael Shadle

**Acquisition Editor**

Usha Iyer

**Commissioning Editors**

Sruthi Kutty

Priyanka Shah

**Technical Editor**

Amit Ramadas

**Project Coordinator**

Sneha Modi

**Proofreader**

Kevin McGowan

**Graphics**

Ronak Dhruv

**Production Coordinator**

Melwyn D'sa

**Cover Work**

Melwyn D'sa

**Cover Image**

Valentina Dsilva

# About the Author

**Martin Fjordvald** is a 24-year-old Danish entrepreneur who started his company straight out of high school. Backed by a popular website, he became a jack of all trades having to deal with the business, programming, and marketing side of his business. As the popularity of his website grew, so did the performance requirements of his code and servers, which eventually led to his discovery of nginx in 2008.

Frustrated with the lack of documentation, Martin got involved with the community project to document nginx, and has since written several blog posts and Wiki articles detailing how nginx works. With the improved official documentation he now mostly blogs about advanced subjects and provides support in the nginx IRC channel on Freenode.

I'd like to first of all thank the nginx team for their wonderful piece of software, without which this book would never have happened. I owe all of my knowledge to the dedicated people of #nginx IRC channel for helping me to understand nginx so much better. I'd also like to thank Piotr Sikora, Jonathan Kolb, and Michael Lustfield, especially for their involvement and dedication to the community.

My thanks to Peter Schofield for helping me work through awkward sentences, improper grammar, and being a general sounding board when I was stuck on how to proceed. Furthermore, thanks goes to my family and parents for constantly asking me how the book was coming along, thus preventing me from procrastinating too much, and without their nagging this book would have taken far longer.

# About the Reviewers

**José Miguel Parrella** started using Linux 12 years ago, and to make a living out of it in 2004 he signed his first government contract for Linux systems administration at the age of 17.

He focused on Debian, a project he joined as a maintainer, then a developer since 2007, for several packages including the nginx Web Server. He has helped government and private customers in several Latin American countries to deploy open source solutions with special attention on Perl-based solutions and clustering, including the Canaima Operating System, a Debian-based distribution used in 2.5M laptops in Venezuela.

For the past three years he has been on an assignment as an Open Source Strategist for a large multinational software company. Born in Venezuela, he is currently based in Washington.

> I'd like to thank a businesswoman I admire, Ailé, who is also my wife and partner, for her unconditional support in all my professional activities.

**Michael Shadle** is a self-proclaimed surgeon, when it comes to procedural PHP. He has been using PHP for over 10 years, along with MySQL and various Linux and BSD distributions. He has switched between many different web servers over the years, and considers nginx to be the best solution yet.

During the day, he works as a senior Web Developer at Intel Corporation on a handful of public-facing websites. He enjoys using his breadth of knowledge to come up with out of the box solutions to solve the variety of issues that come up. During the off-hours, he has a thriving personal consulting and web-development practice. He also has more personal project ideas than he can tackle at once.

He is a minimalist by heart, and believes that when architecting solutions, starting small and simple allows for a more agile approach in the long run. Michael also coined the phrase, "A simple stack is a happy stack."

You can visit his personal blog at `http://michaelshadle.com/`.

# www.packtpub.com

## Support files, eBooks, discount offers and more

You might want to visit www.packtpub.com for support files and downloads related to your book.

Did you know that Packt offers eBook versions of every book published, with PDF and ePub files available? You can upgrade to the eBook version at www.packtpub.com and as a print book customer, you are entitled to a discount on the eBook copy. Get in touch with us at service@packtpub.com for more details.

At www.packtpub.com, you can also read a collection of free technical articles, sign up for a range of free newsletters and receive exclusive discounts and offers on Packt books and eBooks.

# packtlib.packtpub.com

Do you need instant solutions to your IT questions? PacktLib is Packt's online digital book library. Here, you can access, read and search across Packt's entire library of books.

## Why Subscribe?

- ✦ Fully searchable across every book published by Packt
- ✦ Copy and paste, print and bookmark content
- ✦ On demand and accessible via web browser

## Free Access for Packt account holders

If you have an account with Packt at www.packtpub.com, you can use this to access PacktLib today and view nine entirely free books. Simply use your login credentials for immediate access.

# Table of Contents

# Instant Nginx Starter

Welcome to *Instant Nginx Starter*. With this book I aim to give you a solid start to your nginx adventure. You will learn the basic features of nginx and be guided through your first virtual host to a point where you will know how to build on top of the basics to get to advanced features.

This book contains the following sections:

*So, what is nginx?* teaches you what nginx actually is, how it can be used, and how it fares against similar technologies.

*Installation* helps us learn the procedure to download and install nginx with different methods, and the cons and pros of each.

*Quick start* covers nginx configuration syntax while creating our first virtual host through some simple steps. After this section you will be comfortable with the working of an nginx configuration.

*Top 9 features you need to know about* helps you learn to perform nine useful tasks that the nginx modules offer. By the end of this section, you will be able to:

- ✦ G-zip assets for optimal page load time
- ✦ Pre-zip assets for optimal page load time
- ✦ Use nginx as a micro cache
- ✦ How to use WebSockets with nginx
- ✦ Use nginx with other software
- ✦ Set up backend authentication for nginx downloads
- ✦ Do GeoIP lookups in nginx
- ✦ Limiting user requests to prevent abuse
- ✦ Create seekable video streaming with nginx

*People and places you should get to know* provides you with many useful links to resources about nginx, while keeping in mind that the community is important to nginx and it's where most support happens and where a lot of module development takes place.

# So, what is nginx?

The best way to describe nginx (pronounced engine-x) is as an event-based multi-protocol reverse proxy. This sounds fancy, but it's not just buzz words and actually affects how we approach configuring nginx. It also highlights some of the flexibility that nginx offers. While it is often used as a web server and an HTTP reverse proxy, it can also be used as an IMAP reverse proxy or even a raw TCP reverse proxy. Thanks to the plug-in ready code structure, we can utilize a large number of first and third party modules to implement a diverse amount of features to make nginx an ideal fit for many typical use cases.

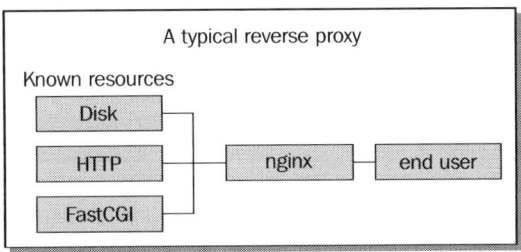

A more accurate description would be to say that nginx is a reverse proxy first, and a web server second. I say this because it can help us visualize the request flow through the configuration file and rationalize how to achieve the desired configuration of nginx. The core difference this creates is that nginx works with URIs instead of files and directories, and based on that determines how to process the request. This means that when we configure nginx, we tell it what should happen for a certain URI rather than what should happen for a certain file on the disk.

A beneficial part of nginx being a reverse proxy is that it fits into a large number of server setups, and can handle many things that other web servers simply aren't designed for. A popular question is "Why even bother with nginx when Apache httpd is available?"

The answer lies in the way the two programs are designed. The majority of Apache setups are done using prefork mode, where we spawn a certain amount of processes and then embed our dynamic language in each process. This setup is synchronous, meaning that each process can handle one request at a time, whether that connection is for a PHP script or an image file.

In contrast, nginx uses an asynchronous event-based design where each spawned process can handle thousands of concurrent connections. The downside here is that nginx will, for security and technical reasons, not embed programming languages into its own process - this means that to handle those we will need to reverse proxy to a backend, such as Apache, PHP-FPM, and so on. Thankfully, as nginx is a reverse proxy first and foremost, this is extremely easy to do and still allows us major benefits, even when keeping Apache in use.

Let's take a look at a use case where Apache is used as an application server described earlier rather than just a web server. We have embedded PHP, Perl, or Python into Apache, which has the primary disadvantage of each request becoming costly. This is because the Apache process is kept busy until the request has been fully served, even if it's a request for a static file. Our online service has gotten popular and we now find that our server cannot keep up with the increased demand. In this scenario introducing nginx as a spoon-feeding layer would be ideal. When an nginx server with a spoon-feeding layer will sit between our end user and Apache and a request comes in, nginx will reverse proxy it to Apache if it is for a dynamic file, while it will handle any static file requests itself. This means that we offload a lot of the request handling from the expensive Apache processes to the more lightweight nginx processes, and increase the number of end users we can serve before having to spend money on more powerful hardware.

Another example scenario is where we have an application being used from all over the world. We don't have any static files so we can't easily offload a number of requests from Apache. In this use case, our PHP process is busy from the time the request comes in until the user has finished downloading the response. Sadly, not everyone in the world has fast internet and, as a result, the sending process could be busy for a relatively significant period of time. Let's assume our visitor is on an old 56k modem and has a maximum download speed of 5 KB per second, it will take them five seconds to download a 25 KB gzipped HTML file generated by PHP. That's five seconds where our process cannot handle any other request. When we introduce nginx into this setup, we have PHP spending only microseconds generating the response but have nginx spend five seconds transferring it to the end user. Because nginx is asynchronous it will happily handle other connections in the meantime, and thus, we significantly increase the number of concurrent requests we can handle.

In the previous two examples I used scenarios where nginx was used in front of Apache, but naturally this is not a requirement. nginx is capable of reverse proxying via, for instance, FastCGI, UWSGI, SCGI, HTTP, or even TCP (through a plugin) enabling backends, such as PHP-FPM, Gunicorn, Thin, and Passenger.

# Installation

There are two ways to install nginx, either by building it from source, or by installing a binary package via a package manager, such as yum or apt. Each method has its own pros and cons, and which method we choose depends on what we need nginx to do and which OS we're using.

Historically nginx, Inc has only provided the source files for nginx so that we could compile the software ourselves, and only recently have they begun distributing binary packages for the various Linux distributions. Additionally, nginx requires that third party modules are compiled statically instead of being loaded at runtime. The end result of this is that the nginx ecosystem ends up with a number of native binary packages and custom binary packages built by different people to include different modules.

Even today many of the Linux distributions ship very old versions of nginx, which means we'll have to be careful when we install nginx to make sure we get the version we need. If we need any third party modules enabled, we are almost guaranteed to have to build from source. Thankfully, nginx is easy to install from source and this book details how to do it without suffering a nervous breakdown.

A last note before we continue to the installation process. nginx has three versions available: development, stable, and legacy. Development here refers to the program API stability, not runtime stability. This means that the development version is usually just as stable, or even more stable than the stable branch. This is because bug fixes are added to the development branch before the stable branch. In general, if I personally want features in a new development version, I will give it a week or two to be tested by the community and then feel safe upgrading to it. Legacy versions should be avoided, as they are not supported by either nginx, Inc or the community, and usually bugs are fixed by simply updating to the stable or development version.

## Step 1 – Different operating systems

Now, we will have a look at installing nginx on different operating systems.

### Windows

Installing on Windows is the easiest of them all, as it's really only available as a binary file unless we want to start compiling through Cygwin, for most people this is overkill. Instead, just head to the nginx download page and get one of the Windows releases as signified by **nginx/Windows-1.X.XX**. Extract that anywhere and we're ready to go!

A word of warning about nginx on Windows though. Windows has a unique version of event polling called IOCP and nginx does not currently support this. This means that nginx falls back to a slower variant, which means that nginx on Windows is not at the same performance standard as nginx on Linux. Additionally, there are a number of limitations that we should be aware of. At the time of writing the following are the known limitations:

+ Only one worker will be used
+ A worker can handle no more than 1,024 concurrent connections
+ Cache modules do not work on Windows Vista or later

nginx, Inc maintains an updated list of known limitations at the following URL:

```
http://www.nginx.org/en/docs/windows.html
```

# Linux

To install on Linux we first need to decide whether we'll compile from source or install via a binary package. To help decide, here's a brief overview of the pros and cons:

### Installation via source

The pros of installing nginx on Linux via source are as follows:

+ It can easily use third party modules
+ It can use the latest version immediately

The cons of installing nginx on Linux via source are as follows:

+ It is more difficult than installing a binary package
+ You have to keep on top of updates yourself

### Installation via binary package

The pros of installing nginx on Linux via binary package are as follows:

+ It is very easy to install
+ You don't have to keep track of updates yourself

The cons of installing nginx on Linux via binary package are as follows:

+ It is difficult to find a binary package with third party modules
+ It is potentially lagging behind on versions
+ It has many different versions, need to research them

Ultimately I personally think it comes down to whether or not you need third party modules. Finding binary packages that contain the modules you need is often difficult and you rely on external people to keep their binary package updated. Compiling from source if you need third party modules also means that we can restrict binary packages to the official nginx provided repositories. This makes it far easier and reduces the research required into the various custom repositories and **Ubuntu Personal Package Archives (PPAs)**.

## Installing from source

Installing nginx from source is not as daunting as it might sound, as nginx is a fairly simple piece of software and we can still utilize yum and apt-get to simplify the installation of the dependencies.

If using apt, simply run the following:

```
sudo apt-get build-dep nginx
```

To automatically install the dependencies for their nginx package, usually these are the same as for what we will install.

If using yum, run the following:

```
sudo yum install pcre-devel zlib-devel openssl-devel
```

At this point we have the dependencies and are ready to compile nginx. Make sure we're in the directory we want to download the source code into and then run the following:

```
wget http://www.nginx.org/download/nginx-1.3.15.tar.gz
tar zxf nginx-1.3.15.tar.gz
cd nginx-1.3.15
./configure --help
```

After running the last command we should get a large amount of text on the screen. If you're not used to compiling from source, this would probably be pretty daunting at first, but let's read through the important points.

| | |
|---|---|
| `--prefix` | This sets the base path where nginx is installed. If not defined, this will default to `/usr/local/nginx`. |
| `--sbin-path` | This sets the path where the binary file is installed. |
| `--conf-path` | This sets the path of the configuration file. |

Any of the other install specific switches can be configured in the configuration file, so those really aren't important to set yet. Further down we start seeing switches named as —with-* and —without-*. Each of these allow us to define which standard modules go into our compiled binary package, and the switches we use depend on which features we want. Each module we include increases the size of the binary package, which increases memory usage. Although, even if we include all the modules, the memory size won't be more than a few megabytes. Do note that some modules might have other dependencies, for instance the GeoIP module relies on external GeoIP software which will have to be installed through your package manager. To read about what each module does, please refer to the official documentation at: http://www. nginx.org/en/docs/.

Once we have decided the modules we want to be included, simply run the following:

```
./configure —with-foo
```

If all the dependencies are correct, a summary screen should be presented as follows:

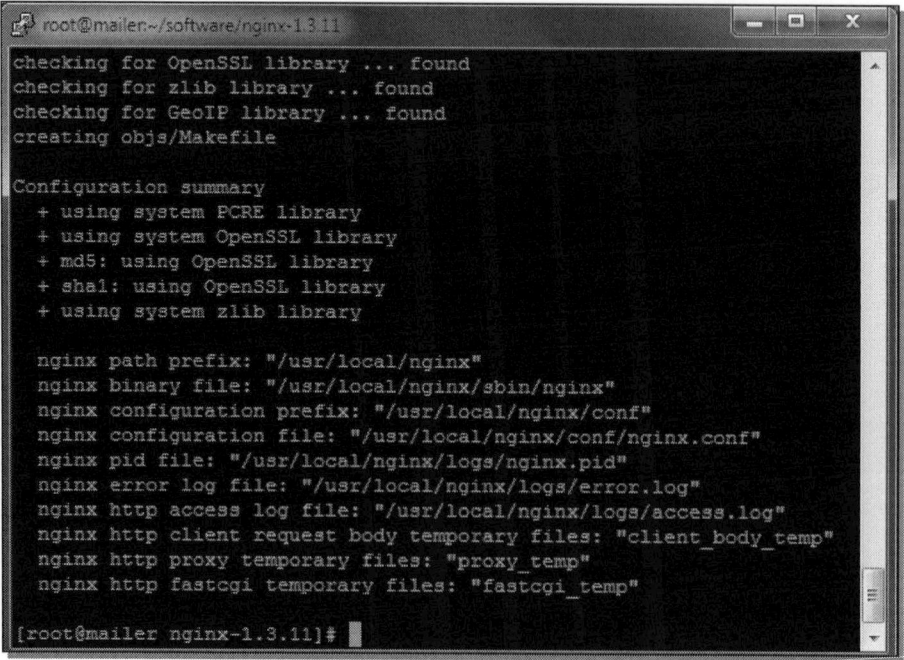

If the information there is as expected, complete the compile by running the follow commands:

```
make
```

```
make install
```

If we already have nginx installed, we can have the make script automatically and seamlessly rotate the running binary package by using the following command:

`make upgrade`

If we did everything right, we should get the following message after running `make install`:

`make[1]: Leaving directory '/path/to/nginx-1.3.15'`

The quickest way to install from a binary package is to simply use the native packages and run either of the following:

`yum install nginx`

or

`apt-get install nginx`

If the version installed is fairly recent, we might want to do just that for convenience, if it's old then move on and use the nginx provided binary packages. To use these first install the repository like so.

For yum:

Create the file `/etc/yum.repos.d/nginx.repo` and add the following to it:

```
 [nginx]
name=nginx repo
baseurl=http://nginx.org/packages/OS/OSRELEASE/$basearch/
gpgcheck=0
enabled=1
```

Where `OS` is *centos* if CentOS is used and *rhel* if RHEL, or another RHEL-based distribution is used. `OSRELEASE` is the OS version number, being either *5* or *6*. If unsure check `uname -a` for a clue, or use the tried and tested method of trial and error.

For apt:

Add the following to `/etc/apt/sources.list` for Debian:

```
deb http://nginx.org/packages/debian/ squeezenginx
deb-src http://nginx.org/packages/debian/ squeezenginx
```

For Ubuntu, add the following:

```
deb http://nginx.org/packages/ubuntu/ codenamenginx
deb-src http://nginx.org/packages/ubuntu/ codenamenginx
```

Where codename is one of lucid, oneiric, precise, or quantal, depending on which version is used and then run:

```
apt-get update
apt-get install nginx
```

# Step 2- Starting nginx

Regardless of how nginx was installed, we will most likely want to start it by using a script. Our options are the classic `init.d` script or an `upstart/systemd` script depending on our platform. If nginx was installed via a binary package, one such script should already have been provided for us and can be used by running:

```
service nginx start
```

If nginx was installed via source, we'll need to install the init script ourselves. An nginx community effort to gather `.init` scripts can be found at: `http://wiki.nginx.org/ InitScripts`, which will help us get set up quickly.

Download the `init` script for the relevant platform and save it to `/etc/rc.d/init.d/ nginx`, check the paths in the `.init` file to make sure they fit the install configurations we set with the `./configure arguments` (or the defaults!), and then run the following:

```
chmod +x /etc/rc.d/init.d/nginx
```

Now run the preceding command up above to see the options available.

# And that's it

At this point nginx should be installed and ready to be configured. It's time to experiment a bit and learn the good stuff!

# Quick start – Creating your first virtual host

It's finally time to get nginx up and running. To start out, let's quickly review the configuration file. If you installed via a system package, the default configuration file location is most likely /etc/nginx/nginx.conf. If you installed via source and didn't change the path prefix, nginx installs itself into /usr/local/nginx and places nginx.conf in a /conf subdirectory. Keep this file open as a reference to help visualize many of the things described in this chapter.

## Step 1 – Directives and contexts

To understand what we'll be covering in this section, let me first introduce a bit of terminology that the nginx community at large uses. Two central concepts to the nginx configuration file are those of **directives** and **contexts**. A directive is basically just an identifier for the various configuration options. Contexts refer to the different sections of the nginx configuration file. This term is important because the documentation often states which context a directive is allowed to have within.

A glance at the standard configuration file should reveal that nginx uses a layered configuration format where blocks are denoted by curly brackets { }. These blocks are what are referred to as contexts.

The topmost context is called main, and is not denoted as a block but is rather the configuration file itself. The main context has only a few directives we're really interested in, the two major ones being worker_processes and user. These directives handle how many worker processes nginx should run and which user/group nginx should run these under.

Within the main context there are two possible subcontexts, the first one being called **events**. This block handles directives that deal with the event-polling nature of nginx. Mostly we can ignore every directive in here, as nginx can automatically configure this to be the most optimal; however, there's one directive which is interesting, namely worker_connections. This directive controls the number of connections each worker can handle. It's important to note here that nginx is a terminating proxy, so if you HTTP proxy to a backend, such as Apache httpd, that will use up two connections.

The second subcontext is the interesting one called http. This context deals with everything related to HTTP, and this is what we will be working with almost all of the time. While there are directives that are configured in the http context, for now we'll focus on a subcontext within http called server. The server context is the nginx equivalent of a virtual host. This context is used to handle configuration directives based on the host name your sites are under.

Within the server context, we have another subcontext called location. The location context is what we use to match the URI. Basically, a request to nginx will flow through each of our contexts, matching first the server block with the hostname provided by the client, and secondly the location context with the URI provided by the client.

Depending on the installation method, there might not be any server blocks in the `nginx.conf` file. Typically, system package managers take advantage of the include directive that allows us to do an in-place inclusion into our configuration file. This allows us to separate out each virtual host and keep our configuration file more organized. If there aren't any server blocks, check the bottom of the file for an `include` directive and check the directory from which it includes, it should have a file which contains a server block.

## Step 2 – Define your first virtual hosts

Finally, let us define our first server block!

```
server {
    listen 80;
    server_name example.com;

    root /var/www/website;
}
```

**Downloading the example code**

You can download the example code files for all Packt books you have purchased from your account at `http://www.packtpub.com`. If you purchased this book elsewhere, you can visit `http://www.packtpub.com/support` and register to have the files e-mailed directly to you.

That is basically all we need, and strictly speaking, we don't even need to define which port to listen on as port 80 is default. However, it's generally a good practice to keep it in there should we want to search for all virtual hosts on port 80 later on.

# Quick start – Interacting with backends

Obviously, this virtual host is quite boring, all it does is serve a static file, and while that is certainly useful, it's practically never all we want to do. Something more interesting would be to serve PHP requests, perhaps even for a framework with a front controller pattern and search engine friendly URLs.

## Step 1 – A quick backend communication example

Communicating with a backend is done by passing the request to the backend if certain conditions are met. For example, in the following server block:

```
server {
    listen 80;
    server_name example.com;

    root /var/www/website;
    index index.php;

    location / {
        try_files $uri $uri/ /index.php;
    }

    location ~ \.php$ {
        include fastcgi.conf;
        fastcgi_pass 127.0.0.1:9000;
    }
}
```

Here we are using a regular expression location block to define what should happen when a request with a URI ending in .php comes in. If the URI does not end in .php but, for instance, / contact-us/, location / is used instead that tries to find a file on the disk using our root directive and the URI. If that's not found, it tries to search for a directory instead and uses our index directive to find an index file. If that is not found either, then it finally rewrites internally to /index.php and restarts location evaluation with the URI now ending in .php and as such the PHP location will be used and send the request to PHP.

## Step 2 – Location blocks

As we'll pass requests to a backend by using location blocks, it'll be useful to understand the different types of location blocks available. Did you notice in the preceding section how the location blocks use different modifiers before the URI? In the first location there is no modifier, and in the second a ~ is used. This modifier changes how nginx matches the location to the URI sent by the end user. The modifiers and rules are as follows:

| Modifier | Result |
|---|---|
| No modifier | This will match as a prefix value. `location /` will match any URI beginning with /, while `location /foo` will match any URI beginning with /foo. |
| = | This will match as an exact value. `location = /foo` will only match the exact URI /foo not the URI /foobar or even /foo/. |
| ~ | This will match as a case sensitive regular expression using the PCRE library. |
| ~* | This will match as a case insensitive regular expression using the PCRE library. |
| ^~ | Will match as a prefix value, which is more important than a regular expression. |

With all of these different location modifiers, nginx needs a way to know which one to use if multiple matches occur. To do this nginx assigns each type of modifier a certain specificity, which helps to determine how important a location is.

| Modifier | Specificity |
|---|---|
| = | This is the most specific modifier possible, as it matches only the exact string. If this location matches, it will be chosen first. |
| ^~ | This modifier is used specifically when you want a prefix match to be more important than a regular expression location. If you have multiple matching locations of this type, the longest match will be used. |
| ~ and ~* | nginx has no way to decide how specific a regular expression is, so these are matched in the order they are defined. This means that if multiple regular expression locations match, the first one defined will be used. |
| No modifier | Finally if nothing else matches, a standard prefix match is used. If multiple prefix locations match, the longest match will be used. |

Knowing how nginx chooses a location is quite essential because of how nginx inheritance works. The common thing with every directive is that it will only ever inherit downwards, never up and never across contexts. In effect this means that we cannot have nginx apply two locations at the same time. As soon as we internally rewrite a request and locations are re-evaluated, nginx will forget about the directives in the old location and only care about the ones in the new location.

For an illustration of this behavior, see this following server block:

```
server {
    root /home/bill/www;
    index index.php;

    location /phpmyadmin {
        root /var/www;
        try_files $uri /phpmyadmin/index.php;
    }

    location ~* \.php$ {
        fastcgi_pass php_upstream;
    }
}
```

When a request comes in for /phpmyadmin/image/foo.jpg, the /phpmyadmin location will be considered most specific and try_files will find the image. In contrast, if a request comes in for /phpmyadmin, it will first use the /phpmyadmin location and then try_files will rewrite the request into the PHP location. When this happens everything from the previous location is discarded and now the root is inherited from the server context making the root /home/bill/www instead, and the request results in a 404 error.

Instead, what we need to do here is use a sublocation so that nginx does not have to inherit across.

```
server {
    root /home/bill/www;
    index index.php;

    location ^~ /phpmyadmin {
        root /var/www;

        location ~* \.php$ {
            fastcgi_pass php_upstream;
        }
    }

    location ~* \.php$ {
```

```
        fastcgi_pass php_upstream;
    }
}
```

In this example we don't need `try_files`, as we have no need to rewrite the request. If the URI matches `/phpmyadmin/`, it will be chosen before the PHP location at the bottom, and if it then also matches the PHP sublocation, it will flow into that one, maintaining the root directive from the parent location.

The positive aspect of the preceding scenario is that it will always be simple to tell which directives will apply to any given request, by just following the rewrites to the final location and checking directives in the parent contexts. There are no complicated inheritance paths across contexts with some values being overridden by new directives, while others persist.

Related to location blocks is something called a **named location**. A named location is essentially a location that isn't reached via the URI, but rather by internal references. A named location is denoted by a @.

```
    location @error404 { … }
```

This location is useful when you want to logically separate out some directives, but don't want that part of the config accessible through the URI. The previously named location might be used for an error page, for example, where it would only be called when a request would result in a 404 error.

```
    error_page 404 @error404;
```

## Step 3 – Directive types

In nginx, a directive will usually inherit based on a simple `http-server-location` flow. Mostly, anyway. nginx has different types of directives and each type inherits a bit differently. How a directive inherits depends on its type. In nginx, there are three types of directives and `try_files`. The three types are as follows:

✦ The standard directive

✦ The array directive

✦ The action directive

The vast majority of directives are **standard directives**. These are passive configuration directives that do nothing but configure some aspect of nginx. They follow the standard inheritance of nginx and inherit downwards unless the lower context specifies the same directive.

**Array directives** differ a bit, as multiple directives can be specified in the same context. An example of an array directive would be the `access_log` directive. If we use the array directive three times in the same location block, nginx will create all three access logs.

The possible confusion with array directives comes from the fact that while we can use the directive multiple times in the same context, when we try to use it multiple times in two different contexts, the lower context will replace the higher one, not add to it. Consider the following example:

```
server {
    access_log /var/log/nginx/access.log;

    location ~ ^/calendar/.+\.php$ {
        access_log /var/log/nginx/php-requests.log;
    }
}
```

In the preceding example, there are two access logs defined but only one of them will ever be written to, depending upon whether the PHP location matches or not. If the goal is to log to both the server context access log and the PHP specific one, we need to define the server context access log twice.

```
server {
    access_log /var/log/nginx/access.log;

    location ~ ^/calendar/.+\.php$ {
        access_log /var/log/nginx/access.log;
        access_log /var/log/nginx/php-requests.log;
    }
}
```

The final type of directive is the action directive. These are directives that cause an immediate action, and as such do not inherit but rather execute immediately if the relevant context becomes active. Take, for example, the `rewrite` directive in the following example:

```
server {
    rewrite ^/booking(.*) /calendar$1;

    location /calendar {
        rewrite ^ /index.php;
    }
}
```

Here the `rewrite` directive in the `server` context will always execute, thus the regex parser will always start and see if the pattern `^/booking(.*)` matches the current URI; the request will then flow into the `/calendar` location and the next rewrite will trigger.

Finally, there's `try_files`, which is a bit of an outlier. This is because `try_files` does not fit any of the other directive types. It is perhaps closest to an action directive in the sense that it will not inherit, the difference is that when placed in the `server` context nginx actually creates a special pseudo-location that is the least specific location possible. This essentially means that `try_files` in the `server` context will only ever execute if no location matches the request. This if of course a possible scenario, however, if `location /` is used, this location will always match and thus `try_files` is never used. It's highly recommended that `try_files` is never placed outside a location, so as to avoid confusion if suddenly `try_files` no longer executes when the configuration is changed.

Unfortunately, this behavior only holds true when we consider the contexts `http-server-location`. Locations can have three different subcontexts of nested location, if-in-location and `limit_except`. The bad news here is that how directive inheritance works for these contexts is entirely up to the module that defines the directive. The good news is that the modules included with nginx have a standardized behavior and that standard and array directives function much like they normally do. The only real difference is with action directives which not only won't inherit, but also won't execute if a nested location matches. The following example illustrates this scenario:

```
server {
    location /calendar {
        rewrite ^ /static.php;

        location ~ \.php$ {
            fastcgi_pass php_upstream;
        }
    }
}
```

The `rewrite` directive in the outer location will execute only if the inner location does not match.

## Step 4 – Location reevaluation

A useful thing to talk about when following action directives is the effect these directives have when executed, as they cause an internal rewrite. With every internal rewrite nginx will reevaluate the locations and possibly select a new one. Keeping internal redirects simple and few in number can often result in less debugging when problems arise.

It's useful to know that while `try_files` was listed as similar to action directives, only the final argument to `try_files` will actually cause a location reevaluation. This can cause issues with `try_files` like this:

```
try_files $uri $uri.php /index.php;
```

While initially this may seem to enable pretty URLs, it will actually cause nginx to potentially output the source code of PHP files to the user, as $uri.php is not the last argument to try_files, and will therefore only set the internal $uri pointer and not reevaluate locations.

Another useful thing to know is that rewrites can be made to not trigger location reevaluation by using the break flag at the end, for example, if you wish to rewrite from an old PHP script to a new one, you can avoid nginx going through the entire location evaluation process again.

```
location ~ \.php$ {
    rewrite ^/old.php /new.php break;
    fastcgi_pass php_upstream;
}
```

## Step 5 – Dealing with backends

Backends come into play once we need to use nginx for something more than just static file serving. nginx is designed to not embed anything within itself, but rather use transport protocols to talk to backends. There are multiple protocols available, such as HTTP, FastCGI, uWSGI, SCGI, and Memcached. Third party plugins may add even more possible protocols, allowing nginx to talk to more different backends.

As nginx separates itself from backends using transport protocols, the management of these backends becomes a separate issue as well.

In order to have nginx talk to a backend, we'll have to tell the backend which file to execute as well as provide it some other information. Thankfully, nginx provides configuration for this with its default install. Check for files fastcgi.conf, uwsgi_params, and scgi_params.

For HTTP proxying we usually need to provide the backend with some information through HTTP headers. Most backends will expect the HOST header to be set as well as the end user IP. Typically, a configuration for proxying would look like the following:

```
location /proxy {
    proxy_set_header HOST $http_host;
    proxy_set_header X-Forwarded-For $remote_addr;
    proxy_pass http://127.0.0.1:8080;
}
```

## Step 6 – What can you do if you get stuck?

Getting stuck is an inevitable part of dealing with servers. The information from the *Step 5 – Dealing with backends* section will help us understand the flow of a request, and thus allow us to know which directives apply to the request. Sometimes, though, it's nice with a bit more information to help us debug a problem faster. For this nginx provides the error log. Most errors go in the error log, even if its a 404 error, or the backend reporting an error. Therefore, it's critical to have an error log defined with a proper log level.

The error log directive in nginx is defined as:

```
error_log file | stderr [debug | info | notice | warn | error | crit |
alert | emerg];
```

When faced with a problem, the first thing to do is set the log level to info and check for any entry in the error log. Usually, there will be something to give a clue, for instance if a 404 error occurs where it shouldn't, the nginx error log will explain where it's trying to find the file and that can help us visualize where in our configuration we've gone wrong.

If things still aren't making sense at this point, nginx offers one more easy way to look at a request. The return directive allows us to return a status code and a string. For instance, we use the following:

```
return 200 $fastcgi_script_name;
```

We can get the content of that variable output. This can function as a poor man's debugger.

# Top 9 features you need to know about

While nginx at the core is designed to be a standard reverse proxy and HTTP web server, we can take it much further and use nginx as a central part in our toolchain, if we look into some of the more esoteric modules as well as the ones not included in the default compile. Thankfully, these modules are very often included in the binary packages provided by repositories, so regardless of which method was used to install nginx, they should be available for us to play with.

Compressing site assets is one of the most important methods to optimize the perceived load time of a first time visitor, and even for subsequent page loads when compressing the HTML backend response.

## Gzipping

Gzipping the JavaScript, CSS, and HTML responses is of utmost importance if load time is considered important, which naturally means that nginx offers this as a core feature. If we include the optional gzip static module, we can optimize this process even further by compressing the assets ahead of time, so that nginx can merely serve the static gzip file instead of having to compress it on-the-fly.

To start off with, let's look at how to enable normal on-the-fly gzip compression.

```
gzip              on;
gzip_min_length   100;
gzip_proxied      expired no-cache no-store private auth;
gzip_comp_level   5;
gzip_types        text/plain text/css text/xml text/javascript
application/xml application/xml+rss application/x-javascript image/x-
icon;
gzip_disable      "msie6";
```

These directives are valid in an `http` context, which means that if we specify them in the `http` block they will apply to every `server` block, thus enabling us to specify compression only once. Using our knowledge of **nginx inheritance** from the *Quick Start* section we can still override this on a server or location basis if required by simply setting the `gzip` directive to `off`.

The different directives are as always explained in detail in the documentation; however, here's a brief overview of what each does:

| Directive | Description |
| --- | --- |
| gzip | On or off, that is enables or disables gzipping. |
| gzip_min_length | This is the minimum response size in bytes before nginx will compress the response. It Defaults to 20 bytes. |
| gzip_proxied | This defines if nginx should compress the response when nginx is behind other proxy software, such as Varnish or HAProxy. It defaults to off. |
| gzip_comp_level | This defines the gzip compression level, default being 1. It gives diminishing returns past level 4, and past level 5 there's rarely any difference at all. Higher levels use more CPU resources. |
| gzip_types | The mime types to compress. Text/html is always compressed if gzipping is enabled. To compress everything use *, though, this also compresses resources which are already compressed, thus wasting server resources. |
| gzip_disable | Regex matched against the user agent to determine when to not compress in case the user agent is buggy. msie6 is a special value for Internet Explorer 4 to 6, which were buggy. |

## Pre-gzipping

Using the pre-gzipping module has the advantage of saving CPU resources, as the site assets will already be stored in a compressed format instead of having to be compressed on each request. Making use of the pre-gzipping module is both simpler and more complicated at the same time. More complicated as we have to gzip the files ourselves, but simpler as there are far less configuration directives. To enable the precompressed gzip module we simply use the following configuration:

```
gzip_static      on;
gzip_proxied     expired no-cache no-store private auth;
gzip_disable     "msie6";
```

Immediately, we'll see that the only new directive is really gzip_static which, like the gzip directive, takes an on or off value to enable or disable it.

Gzipping files is a bit outside the scope of this book. It can either be done by hand using the command line gzip application, or automated as part of a build process, but it has to be done outside of nginx.

# Using nginx as a full-page micro cache

It's noon and you've just sat down for lunch when your monitoring service sends you a text message saying your start-up's newly launched web service is down. Seconds later your cofounder texts you in a panic that the website is down, and just as his submissions to HackerNews and Reddit got on the front page too. Ars Technica and The Next Web are currently writing articles covering your start-up and the world is literally about to go under if you don't get the website online immediately.

Enter the micro cache. The concept is that any page which doesn't contain user specific information should be cached in nginx, so that the backend application isn't even touched. This relieves load on the backend and allows most applications to handle far more traffic. Normally, an application will have to be written with caching in mind to handle invalidation of cached pages whenever content updates. The micro cache concept handles this by only caching things for a short period of time. If traffic spikes to 20 requests per second, and the micro cache is set to expire after 10 seconds, that's 200 requests the backend application did not have to handle, which makes micro caching a good tool to use when in a pinch.

While the concept of micro cache is simple, the execution can be a bit more complicated depending on the application. The key aspect is to only cache pages that contain no user specific information. If no such thing exists, it's very simple, otherwise we'll need to control when to cache and when not to cache.

There are two approaches to do this. The first is to use the built-in FastCGI cache or the equivalent for the other modules, such as proxy, uWSGI, SCGI, and so on. The second is to use Memcached as a cache, which is agnostic to the proxy method.

The difference between the two methods is that the built-in FastCGI cache is read and write, while Memcached cache is read-only. Essentially, it becomes a question of where the responsibility for writing to the cache lies. With the built-in FastCGI cache the logic is placed in the nginx config, while with Memcached the logic is placed in the application, as it will need to write to the cache itself.

## Memcached micro cache

Lets start with the Memcached scenario, as that's simpler from an nginx point of view and largely similar in construct for us to build on later. A basic Memcached micro cache would look like the following in the nginx configuration:

```
server {
    root /var/www;

    location / {
        try_files $uri /index.php$is_args$args;
    }

    location ~* \.php$ {
```

```
        default_type text/html;
        charset       utf-8;

        if ($request_method = GET) {
            set $memcached_key $request_method$request_uri;

            memcached_pass host:11211;
            error_page       404 502 504 = @nocache;
        }

        if ($request_method != GET) {
            fastcgi_pass backend;
        }
    }

    location @nocache {
        fastcgi_pass backend;
    }
}
```

In the preceding configuration, the important aspects take place inside the location to handle PHP requests. Specifically, the variable $memcached_key is the most important, as this defines the key to request from Memcached.

A potential complication here is if pages with user data and without user data share the same request URI. In this case, extra configuration is needed to check if a page contains user data. This is always application specific, but common methods are checking for cookies via $http_cookie or checking the URL arguments through $args.

Another thing to notice is that only GET requests use the cache, anything not a GET request will instead fastcgi_pass to our backend, thus bypassing the cache.

If a request passes all the validation and is sent to Memcached and Memcached returns a 404 not found status, error_page will send the request to the @nocache named location, which will fastcgi_pass to our backend. The backend is then responsible for populating the proper key in Memcached for the next request to use.

As the application is writing to the cache here, remember to set the cache expire time to something low enough that we won't have stale cache entries for long when the application date updates.

# Built-in FastCGI cache

Using the built-in caches is very similar in construct to the previous config example. The main difference is that not only do we have to define when to read from the cache, but also when to write to it. A typical configuration would look like the following:

```
fastcgi_cache_path /var/cache/nginx levels=1:2 keys_zone=microcache:5m
max_size=500m;

server {
    root /var/www;

    location / {
        try_files $uri /index.php$is_args$args;
    }

    location ~* \.php$ {
        set $no_cache "";

        # Verify request method is GET or HEAD.
        if ($request_method !~ ^(GET|HEAD)$) {
            set $no_cache "1";
        }

        # Check if a nocache cookie is set, for instance after
handling a POST.
        if ($http_cookie ~* "_nocache") {
            set $no_cache "1";
        }

        fastcgi_no_cache $no_cache;
        fastcgi_cache_bypass $no_cache;

        fastcgi_cache microcache;
        fastcgi_cache_key $request_method$request_uri;

        fastcgi_cache_valid 200 5s;
        fastcgi_cache_use_stale updating;

        fastcgi_pass backend;
    }
}
```

As can be seen, the concept is largely the same. Set up the cache `keys_zone`, figure out whether to cache or not and finally set the cache key. To fully explain what's going on, let's have a look at what the different directives actually do.

| Directive | Description |
| --- | --- |
| `fastcgi_cache_path` | Sets the path to store cached responses under. Also names the key zone associated with this cache path and specifies how much metadata and data can be stored there. In this example, `keys_zone` is called micro cache. |
| `fastcgi_no_cache` | Specifies whether to write to the cache or not. Anything other than an empty string or the value numeric 0 will cause it to not write to the cache. |
| `fastcgi_bypass_cache` | Specifies whether to read from the cache or not. Anything other than an empty string or the numeric value 0 will cause it to not read from the cache. |
| `fastcgi_cache` | Specifies `keys_zone` to use. In this example, the `keys_zone` used is micro cache. |
| `fastcgi_cache_key` | The key used to identify data in the cache. |
| `fastcgi_cache_valid` | Sets the caching time for a given response code. In this example, we want to cache only 200 responses and we will cache them for 5 seconds. Our application can override this directive using the `X-Accel-Expires` header from the X-Accel module or by using standard caching headers `Expires` and `Cache-Control`. |
| `fastcgi_cache_use_stale` | Specifies when the cache will use a cache entry after it's expired. In this example, we use `updating` to allow us to use the cache while it's being updated, thus preventing a sudden flood of connections when a key expires. |

## Using nginx behind other proxies

While nginx can certainly be used as the only reverse proxy in our stack, there are scenarios where we might want to use alternative software in front of nginx because we have in-house expertise or are already using them. Popular choices here are Varnish and HAProxy.

In this case we can have nginx handle such a scenario transparently using the optional module Real IP. With this we can have nginx transparently replace the variables referencing an IP with the IP of the proxy, thus keeping logs and the configuration of the same while giving us the ability to turn frontends on and off.

There are only three directives associated with the real IP module, thus making it fairly simple to implement and understand.

```
set_real_ip_from    192.168.1.0/24;
set_real_ip_from    192.168.2.1;
set_real_ip_from    2001:0db8::/32;
real_ip_header      X-Forwarded-For;
real_ip_recursive on;
```

| Directive | Description |
| --- | --- |
| set_real_ip_from | This specifies an IP to enable the real IP module from. Preventing random people from pretending to be a frontend to nginx. This can be specified multiple times. |
| real_ip_header | This specifies the header to get the real IP from. X-Forwarded-For and X-Real-IP are the most commonly used. This defaults to X-Real-IP. |
| real_ip_recursive | This specifies the IP to use. If off, this will use the last address in header defined by real_ip_header. If on, this will search the IP list until it finds one not in the trusted IP list. This is useful when a request has been forwarded multiple times. This defaults to off. |

## Setting up secure downloads

nginx has a feature called X-Accel which is meant as a replacement for the mod_sendfile functionality found in Apache httpd and lighttpd. The concept is mostly the same. A request is sent to a backend application, which can then do whatever it needs to do, for instance it might log a download or validate user credentials. Once the backend application is done doing its work it issues a non-standard HTTP header X-Accel-Redirect with a path to the file relative to the document root. nginx will detect this header and look for a matching location based on the path sent. An example of this would be a PHP backend application issuing a header X-Accel-Redirect, that is, /video/birthday/dad.mp4.

In nginx, we would then have the following configuration:

```
server {
    root /var/www;

    location /video {
        root /mnt/data;
    }
}
```

In this scenario, nginx would then look for the file at the path `/mnt/data/video/birthday/dad.mp4`. If the file is not found it will send a 404 status error; if the file is found it will start sending the file to the end user, thus relieving the backend application of this.

nginx has a number of X-Accel headers available.

| Header | Description |
| --- | --- |
| X-Accel-Redirect | Specifies a URI relative to the root directive in nginx configuration to the file to send to the user. |
| X-Accel-Buffering | Specifies whether to allow nginx to buffer the connection or not. Turn off if doing Comet style application. Defaults to yes. |
| X-Accel-Charset | Specifies the character set of the connection. Defaults to utf-8. |
| X-Accel-Expires | Used to control whether nginx will cache the application response or not. Defaults to off. |
| X-Accel-Limit-Rate | Specifies a rate limit for the connection. |

## Doing GeoIP lookups

To do a GeoIP lookup, nginx will need the MaxMind GeoIP database. Both the paid and free versions are compatible with this module. The free version can be downloaded from:

```
http://dev.maxmind.com/geoip/geolite
```

Every directive in this module has to be defined in the `http` section and looks like the following:

```
geoip_country          /var/data/GeoIP.dat;
geoip_city             /var/data/GeoLiteCity.dat;
geoip_proxy            192.168.2.0/24;
geoip_proxy_recursive  on;
```

| Directive | Description |
| --- | --- |
| `geoip_country` | Specifies the path to the country level GeoIP database. |
| `geoip_city` | Specifies the path to the city level GeoIP database. This database also contains the data from the country database. |
| `geoip_org` | Specifies the path to the organization level GeoIP database. The GeoIP organization database is a paid-only database that nginx also supports. |
| `geoip_proxy` | When nginx is used behind other proxy software, this can be used to specify the IP of that proxy and have nginx do a lookup on the IP in X-Forwarded-For instead. |
| `geoip_proxy_recursive` | Functionally similar to `real_ip_recursive` from the using nginx behind other proxies example. |

When the proper database is loaded into nginx, the following variables will become available to be used through the config, for instance in the access log or to be passed on to a backend.

| Variable | Description |
| --- | --- |
| `$geoip_country_code`<br>`$geoip_city_country_code` | Variable name depends on the database specified. Contains the two letter country code. |
| `$geoip_country_code3`<br>`$geoip_city_country_code3` | Variable name depends on the database specified. Contains the three letter country code. |
| `$geoip_country_name`<br>`$geoip_city_country_name` | Variable name depends on the database specified. Contains the full country name. |
| `$geoip_city_continent_code` | Contains the two letter code for the continent. Only available in city database. |
| `$geoip_dma_code` | Contains US region DMA code. Only available in city database. |
| `$geoip_latitude` | Contains the latitude of the users location. Only available in city database. |
| `$geoip_longitude` | Contains the longitude of the users location. Only available in city database. |
| `$geoip_region` | Contains the two symbol country region code. Only available in city database. |
| `$geoip_region_name` | Contains the full country region name. Only available in city database. |
| `$geoip_city` | Contains the full city name. Only available in city database. |
| `$geoip_postal_code` | Contains the postal code of the city. Only available in city database. |
| `$geoip_org` | Contains the organization name. Could for instance be a university. Only available in organization database. |

# Limiting user requests

There are two ways to limit requests in nginx, concurrent requests and frequency of requests. Both can be used simultaneously and multiple times on different factors. For instance, we can limit concurrent requests per IP while we limit concurrent requests per server block.

To achieve this, nginx has two modules; one which limits concurrency and the other which limits frequency.

## Limiting concurrent connections

To limit concurrent requests, we use the **limit conn** module. The concept is fairly simple, we create a memory zone based on a variable and nginx will then track concurrent requests grouped by this variable. We could, for instance, use the $server\_name$ variable to limit concurrent requests per vhost, or we could use $binary\_remote\_addr$ to limit on a users IP.

```
limit_conn_zone $binary_remote_addr zone=perip:5m;

server {
    location /download/ {
        limit_conn perip 1;
        limit_conn_log_level error;
    }
}
```

| Directive | Description |
| --- | --- |
| limit_conn_zone | This creates the memory zone. This also specifies the variable to limit based on as well as the maximum size of the memory zone. |
| limit_conn | This specifies which zone to limit by and how many concurrent connections to allow. |
| limit_conn_log_level | This specifies the log level required before the module will log that the concurrent connection limit was exceeded. This defaults to error. Generally, it is not advised to set it lower unless needed, as it can quickly flood the error log and hide more useful data. |

## Limit frequency of connections

To limit the frequency of connections we can use the **limit req** module. It's syntactically similar with only some minor changes to control rate instead of concurrency.

```
limit_req_zone $binary_remote_addr zone=one:5m rate=1r/s;

server {
    location /search/ {
        limit_req zone=one burst=5;
        limit_req_log_level error;
    }
}
```

| Directive | Description |
|---|---|
| limit_req_zone | This creates the memory zone. This specifies the variable to limit based on the variable used as well as the maximum size of the memory zone and the rate at which connections should be allowed. Requests exceeding this rate will be buffered until they reach the limit set by burst at which point they will return 503 instead. |
| limit_req | This specifies which zone to limit by and the size of the request buffer, called **burst**. |
| limit_req_log_level | This specifies the log level required before module will log that the connection frequency limit was exceeded. This defaults to error. Generally, it is not advised to set it lower unless needed, as it can quickly flood the error log and hide more useful data. |

## Using nginx for streaming videos

Streaming videos with nginx is extremely easy. nginx has two optional modules for streaming videos, FLV and MP4, which enable it to stream flash video formats and MP4 containers with H.264/AAC encoding. These modules are compatible with all the traditional Flash and HTML5 players available today.

### Streaming FLV files

The FLV module is the simplest of the two and contains only a single directive. To enable it, simply specify flv in a location as follows:

```
location ~ \.flv$ {
    root /var/www/video;
    flv;
}
```

That's literally everything there is to FLV streaming on the nginx side. If the .flv files are properly prepared with metadata and keyframes, they should stream smoothly and be seekable with this.

### Streaming MP4 files

The MP4 module is pretty much exactly the same with only a few extra directives for additional control.

```
location ~ \.mp4$ {
    root /var/www/video;

    mp4;
    mp4_buffer_size      512k
    mp4_max_buffer_size 10m;
}
```

The buffers control how much memory nginx can use to process the file. This is only limiting during metadata parsing where a large buffer may be required. For this the maximum buffer size becomes relevant. If it's set too small, nginx will output a 500 status error and log the error as:

```
/var/www/video/file.mp4" mp4 moov atom is too large: 12583268, you may
want to increase mp4_max_buffer_size
```

## Using WebSockets with nginx

Version 1.3.13 introduced connection upgrading support to nginx, which means WebSocket support. As WebSockets use the standard HTTP protocol for the initial handshake, nginx can make WebSocket support part of the standard proxy module. This means that all the features available to normal HTTP backends are also available to WebSocket proxying.

The configuration required for handling connection upgrading is as follows:

```
location /chat/ {
    proxy_pass http://backend;
    proxy_http_version 1.1;
    proxy_set_header Upgrade $http_upgrade;
    proxy_set_header Connection "upgrade";
}
```

A few things to notice about WebSocket support are that they can time out just like any other HTTP proxied request. WebSockets are affected by `proxy_read_timeout` that defaults to 60 seconds. The **keepalive** feature in nginx is not of use here, as keepalive pings are empty packets and as such contain no data for nginx to pass to the backend. To combat this, you either need to raise the time out, or implement your own keepalive ping message. The added benefit of the latter solution is that it will also function as a health check for the connection itself.

# People and places you should get to know

The following links are a collection of individuals, aggregating sites, and articles that are worth following for the occasional nugget of nginx wisdom.

## Official links

✦ Website for nginx, Inc, the company behind the nginx software:

    http://nginx.com

✦ Website for the nginx software, includes documentation and links to resources, such as books:

    http://nginx.org

## Articles and tutorials

✦ The following link is community-curated but is also the officially hosted documentation, which sometimes contains additional information compared to official documentation, not always updated, though:

    http://wiki.nginx.org

## Community

✦ A web interface for the mailing list, the only official way to get help:

    http://forum.nginx.org

✦ Community supported IRC channel with high activity:

    Irc://irc.freenode.org/nginx (#nginx channel on irc.freenode.org)

## Blogs

✦ An aggregator of various nginx blogs at:

    http://planet.ngx.cc/

✦ A community supporter who blogs about nginx:

    http://kbeezie.com/tag/nginx/

✦ A community supporter who blogs about nginx:

    http://michael.lustfield.net/category/linux/nginx

◆ Blog of a prolific module creator; mostly writes about his own third party modules but occasionally has insights into nginx internals:

```
http://agentzh.blogspot.com
```

◆ Blog of a module creator, Valery Kholodkov, who also blogs about the internals of nginx:

```
http://www.nginxguts.com/category/nginx/
```

◆ An editorial on the nginx code architecture by Andrew Alexeev of nginx, Inc:

```
http://www.aosabook.org/en/nginx.html
```

◆ A somewhat outdated, but still relevant guide to nginx module development

```
http://www.evanmiller.org/nginx-modules-guide.html
```

◆ A somewhat outdated, but still relevant guide to advanced nginx module development

```
http://www.evanmiller.org/nginx-modules-guide-advanced.html
```

◆ As a community supporter, I blog about nginx at:

```
http://blog.martinfjordvald.com/category/nginx/
```

## Twitter

◆ The official nginx Twitter account:

```
https://twitter.com/nginxorg
```

◆ Core developer of nginx; tends to be active in support channels:

```
https://twitter.com/mdounin
```

◆ My Twitter account is:

```
https://twitter.com/mfjordvald
```

◆ A Twitter search for nginx sometimes reveals some interesting articles:

```
https://twitter.com/search?q=nginx
```

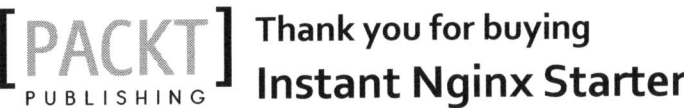

## About Packt Publishing

Packt, pronounced 'packed', published its first book "*Mastering phpMyAdmin for Effective MySQL Management*" in April 2004 and subsequently continued to specialize in publishing highly focused books on specific technologies and solutions.

Our books and publications share the experiences of your fellow IT professionals in adapting and customizing today's systems, applications, and frameworks. Our solution based books give you the knowledge and power to customize the software and technologies you're using to get the job done. Packt books are more specific and less general than the IT books you have seen in the past. Our unique business model allows us to bring you more focused information, giving you more of what you need to know, and less of what you don't.

Packt is a modern, yet unique publishing company, which focuses on producing quality, cutting-edge books for communities of developers, administrators, and newbies alike. For more information, please visit our website: www.packtpub.com.

## Writing for Packt

We welcome all inquiries from people who are interested in authoring. Book proposals should be sent to author@packtpub.com. If your book idea is still at an early stage and you would like to discuss it first before writing a formal book proposal, contact us; one of our commissioning editors will get in touch with you.

We're not just looking for published authors; if you have strong technical skills but no writing experience, our experienced editors can help you develop a writing career, or simply get some additional reward for your expertise.

## Nginx HTTP Server

ISBN: 978-1-84951-086-8        Paperback: 348 pages

Adopt Nginx for your web applications to make the most of your infrastructure and serve pages faster than ever

1. Get started with Nginx to serve websites faster and safer

2. Learn to configure your servers and virtual hosts efficiently

3. Set up Nginx to work with PHP and other applications via FastCGI

4. Explore possible interactions between Nginx and Apache to get the best of both worlds

## Mastering Nginx

ISBN: 978-1-84951-744-7        Paperback: 322 pages

An in-depth guide to configuring NGINX for any situation, including numerous examples and reference tables describing each directive

1. An in-depth configuration guide to help you understand how to best configure NGINX for any situation

2. Includes useful code samples to help you integrate NGINX into your application architecture

3. Full of example configuration snippets, best-practice descriptions, and reference tables for each directive

Please check **www.PacktPub.com** for information on our titles

PUBLISHING

Nginx 1 Web Server
Implementation Cookbook

Over 100 recipes to master using the Nginx HTTP server
and reverse proxy

Dipankar Sarkar

# Nginx 1 Web Server Implementation Cookbook

ISBN: 978-1-84951-496-5        Paperback: 236 pages

Over 100 recipes to master using the Nginx HTTP server
and reverse proxy

1. Quick recipes and practical techniques to help you
   maximize your experience with Nginx

2. Interesting recipes that will help you optimize your
   web stack and get more out of your existing setup

3. Secure your website and prevent your setup from
   being compromised using SSL and rate-limiting
   techniques

IBM Cognos 10
Business Intelligence

A practical approach to all things IBM Cognos 10 Business
Intelligence.

Dustin Adkison

# IBM Cognos 10 Business Intelligence

ISBN: 978-1-84968-356-2        Paperback: 405 pages

A practical approach to all things IBM Cognos 10 Business
Intelligence

1. Learn how to better administer your IBM Cognos 10
   environment in order to improve productivity and
   efficiency.

2. Empower your business with the latest Business
   Intelligence (BI) tools.

3. Discover advanced tools and knowledge that can
   greatly improve daily tasks and analysis.

Please check **www.PacktPub.com** for information on our titles

7412045R00028

Printed in Great Britain
by Amazon.co.uk, Ltd.,
Marston Gate.